Modern Industrial World

Japan

Lesley Downer

Wayland

MODERN INDUSTRIAL WORLD

Austria	**Italy**
Benelux Countries	**Japan**
Canada	**Portugal**
France	**Russia**
Germany	**South Africa**
Ireland	**Spain**
Israel	**Sweden**

JAPAN is dedicated to my nephews, Christopher and James

Cover: The Shinkansen (Bullet Train) hurtles past Mount Fuji.
Title page: Tokyo's Ginza Strip, one of the most famous shopping streets in the world.
Contents page: A rice field in Gifu prefecture, Japan.

Series editor: Paul Mason
Series designer: Malcolm Walker

First published in 1994 by
Wayland (Publishers) Ltd
61 Western Road, Hove
East Sussex, BN3 1JD, England

British Library Cataloguing in Publication Data
Downer, Lesley
   Japan. – (Modern Industrial World Series)
   I. Title II. Series
   952

ISBN 0–7502–0986–0

Typeset by Kudos Design
Printed and bound by G. Canale & C.s.p.A, Turin, Italy

Contents

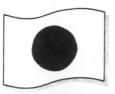

A Land of Contrasts

Left *The bright lights of Tokyo's skyscrapers symbolize the thriving economy of modern Japan.*

The Japanese call their country *Nihon*, which means 'the source of the sun' or 'the land of the rising sun', because it is so far east. It is a land of mountains and lakes, of great cities and skyscrapers. And it is one of the wealthiest and most technologically advanced countries in the world.

The tranquillity of Lake Towada on the island of Honshu is a complete contrast to bustling city life.

Japan lies off the east coast of mainland Asia. Its nearest neighbour, Korea, is less than 300 kilometres away. The country has many links with the mainland. Scholars believe that thousands of years ago the first Japanese people migrated from Korea or China to Japan. Many elements of Japanese culture – the writing system, even the way society is organized – originated in China. Today, too, Japan has close economic and political ties with the rest of the continent.

Japan is in Asia, but it looks to the west. It is one of the countries bordering the Pacific Ocean that are known as the countries of the Pacific Rim. Its strongest ties are with the USA, on the far side of the Pacific.

After the Second World War, the Americans occupied Japan for seven years. While traditional Japanese culture was greatly influenced by China, modern Japanese culture is equally influenced by the USA. The streets of Japanese cities are not very different from those in American cities. Japanese children grow up eating fast food like fish fingers and McDonald's hamburgers, and watching American films. There is even a Disneyland outside Tokyo.

A COUNTRY OF ISLANDS

Altogether there are nearly 4,000 Japanese islands, stretching like a necklace for more than 2,500 kilometres along the edge of Asia. Most people live on the four largest islands. More than three-quarters of Japan's area is uninhabitable, covered in steep, densely forested mountains. Ridge upon ridge of soaring mountains run right along the chain of islands like a spine.

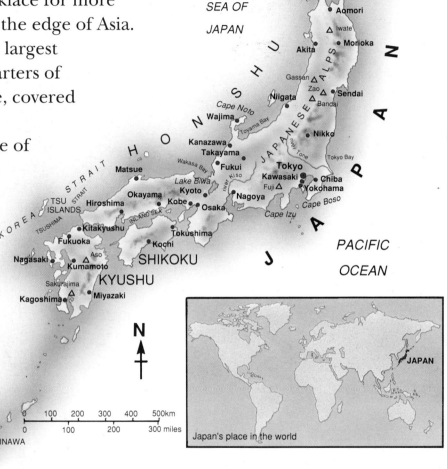

The islands of Japan and their position in the world (inset).

JAPAN AT A GLANCE

Area: 377,737 square kilometres.
Population: 123,610,000.
Capital: Tokyo.
Currency: Yen.
Main cities (population in millions): Tokyo 8.3, Yokohama 3.1, Osaka 2.6, Nagoya 2.1, Sapporo 1.6, Kobe 1.5, Kyoto 1.5, Fukuoka 1.2, Kawasaki 1.1, Kitakyushu 1.0, Hiroshima 1.0.
Religion: Mainly Shinto and Buddhist; also Christian and others.
Highest mountain: Mount Fuji (3,776 metres) on the island of Honshu.

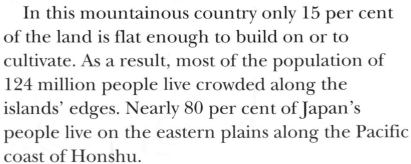

In this mountainous country only 15 per cent of the land is flat enough to build on or to cultivate. As a result, most of the population of 124 million people live crowded along the islands' edges. Nearly 80 per cent of Japan's people live on the eastern plains along the Pacific coast of Honshu.

To the north is the island of Hokkaido. The climate there is cooler, with long, snowy winters, and the landscape is mountainous, with numerous volcanic peaks. Many of the slopes are covered with grass and alpine wildflowers. The island is largely agricultural, given over to sheep, horses and cattle.

Okinawa is one of the Ryukyu chain of islands in the far south of Japan. Because of its tropical climate, it is a popular destination for holidaymakers.

To the south, the island of Shikoku is a quiet backwater, full of picturesque terraced rice fields and beautiful mountains. It is now linked to Honshu by a suspension bridge. As a result, Honshu will probably quickly become more developed.

Development has already spread to Kyushu, the southernmost of the four main islands. Japan's computer and microchip industry is centred there and the island is sometimes called 'Silicon Island' after California's 'Silicon Valley'. The countryside is semi-tropical, with palm trees and two active volcanoes.

CLIMATE

Although there are variations in temperature, all the islands of Japan have four distinct seasons. Winter is cold, with heavy snowfall on the mountains in the north and west of the country. Spring is heralded by the blooming of the cherry trees. Summer is uncomfortably hot and humid.

White cranes blend into a snow-covered field in Hokkaido, Japan's most northerly island.

CLIMATE			
	Min. temp.	Max. temp.	Annual rainfall
Sapporo (Hokkaido)	-4.6 °C	21.7 °C	1,130 mm
Tokyo (Honshu)	5.2 °C	27.1 °C	1,405 mm

Autumn brings typhoons, with fierce winds and drenching rain which often leads to flooding.

EARTHQUAKES

One of the greatest fears in Japan is earthquake. Like California, Japan lies in an earthquake zone, where two plates of the earth's crust meet. There are tremors every day, though most are so small that they are unnoticeable. From time to time there is a much larger tremor. Lights swing, windows rattle and small items fall off shelves.

Tokyo, Japan's capital, lies close to an earthquake epicentre. The Great Earthquake of 1923 destroyed the city and killed over 100,000 people. Experts predict that devastating earthquakes will continue to occur about once every 70 years. The next one was therefore due in 1993; it has yet to come.

All Japanese children learn what to do in the event of an earthquake and have regular earthquake drills at school.

LACK OF NATURAL RESOURCES

Japan has two great problems – a large population and a lack of natural resources. As an industrialized country, Japan needs oil and coal to produce energy. It needs raw materials like iron ore to make iron and steel, as well as copper, zinc, lead, gold and silver. It needs timber for building. But it produces only very small quantities of all of these. Most have to be imported. Much of Japan's food, too, is imported. This makes the country dangerously dependent on the rest of the world. Japan is currently developing nuclear power stations, to reduce its dependence on imported oil and coal.

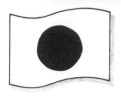

Japan Past and Present

On 30 August 1945 a tall, relaxed American stepped from his plane onto the tarmac at Atsugi airbase in Japan. He was dressed in uniform but wearing no tie, and he was smoking a corncob pipe. His name was General Douglas MacArthur. He was the Supreme Commander for the Allied Powers (SCAP), the leader of the occupying forces. For Japan, his arrival marked the beginning of an entirely new era.

The country MacArthur had come to govern was in ruins at the end of the Second World War (1939-45). It had been utterly defeated after four years of bitter fighting. Every city but one – the historic city of Kyoto – had been flattened by bombing. The people were desperate and on the brink of starvation.

THE EARLY YEARS

The story of modern Japan really began long before General MacArthur stepped from his aeroplane. For over 250 years, from 1603 to 1868, Japan was ruled by military leaders

'Before us, as far as we could see, lay miles of rubble. The people looked ragged and distraught. They dug into the debris, to clear space for new shacks. They pushed and dragged carts piled high with brick and lumber. But so vast was the destruction that all this effort seemed unproductive.'
– Mark Gayn, seeing Tokyo for the first time on 5 December 1945, *Japan Diary*, 1948

General Douglas MacArthur, the American officer who led the occupying forces in Japan after the Second World War.

8

known as shoguns, who kept the country under a system of extremely tight controls. Foreigners were considered a danger to the stability of the state. They were not allowed to enter, and Japanese were not allowed to leave. In the outside world during the nineteenth century, life was changing very fast. Britain was being transformed by the Industrial Revolution. But in Japan very little altered. This stability led to great prosperity and economic growth, which laid the foundations for the future success of the country.

In 1853 four American gunships arrived in Yokohama Bay. Under the leadership of Commodore Perry, the Americans tried to force the Japanese to open their country to trade. The stability of the social system was shaken to its foundations, and as a result the shoguns were overthrown. In 1868 the Emperor Meiji, who was only 16 at the time, regained authority from the shoguns and became the head of state. (This event is known as the Meiji Restoration.)

When Commodore Perry arrived in Yokohama in 1853, he was taken to meet the Japanese Imperial Commissioners.

The Japanese were eager to catch up with the changes that were transforming the West. By 1872, only four years after the emperor took power, they had already built their first railway, with the help of British engineers. Young Japanese went to the West to study, Western experts were invited to Japan to teach. It was a phenomenal period of economic growth. Within a few years the Japanese had built up a number of industries. These were led by several large families who formed conglomerates called *zaibatsu*. By 1905 Japan was so powerful that it was able to defeat Russia, a far larger nation, in a short war.

9

Gradually the power of the army in Japan grew stronger and stronger. When the Second World War broke out in Europe, Japan allied with Germany and on 7 December 1941 attacked the American naval base in Pearl Harbor, Hawaii. From then on all its industries were devoted entirely to weapons production for the war.

Four years later Japan had been defeated. To force the Japanese to surrender, the Allies dropped two atomic bombs, one on the city of Hiroshima, one on Nagasaki. Both were utterly destroyed. Tokyo was bombarded with firebombs and burnt to the ground. There was little left except ashes and the skeletons of ruined buildings.

THE OCCUPATION

General MacArthur's job was to ensure that Japan never went to war again. To do so, he tried to change the entire social system of the country. He drew up a new constitution which stated that 'the Japanese people forever renounce war'. From then on, Japan was to have no army, no navy and no air force. Since the time of Emperor Meiji, the Japanese had been taught that the emperor was divine. General MacArthur's new constitution stated that the emperor was not divine. Instead he was a symbol of the state, a constitutional monarch like the Queen of England.

A Japanese museum worker holds a badly damaged metal clock. It was found in the ruins of Hiroshima after an atomic bomb was dropped on the city in 1945.

'Aspiring sincerely to an international peace based on justice and order, the Japanese people forever renounce war as a sovereign right of the nation and the threat or use of force as means of settling international disputes. In order to accomplish the aim of the preceding paragraph, land, sea, and air forces, as well as other war potential, will never be maintained. The right of belligerency of the state will not be recognized.'
– Article 9 of Japan's peace constitution

One important reform that MacArthur wanted to make was to break up the *zaibatsu*, the large family-run conglomerates which dominated the country's economy. They were extremely powerful; and they had played a large part in supporting the war. A few were broken up, but many retained their power. In the end MacArthur realized that these great businesses would play a vital part in speeding Japan's economic recovery.

THE KOREAN WAR

In 1950 war broke out in Korea. United Nations forces, consisting largely of American troops, were sent to support the South Koreans. For Japan, the Korean War was the turning point. The Americans no longer wanted a quiet, passive Japan. They needed a strong and co-operative ally in Asia. They also needed arms. Japanese factories began producing arms again, to supply the American soldiers fighting in Korea. There was also demand for lorries, tools and spare parts for military equipment and aircraft. As a result, Japanese heavy industry quickly began to expand.

Soon afterwards, in 1952, the Occupation ended, although American troops continued to be stationed in Japan. By the end of the Occupation, thanks to American financial aid and American help, the economy was already much strengthened.

The Shikawajima shipbuilding yard in operation, 1956. Shipbuilding was one of the first industries to be built up by the Japanese government once the Second World War was over.

DEFENCE SPENDING OF MAJOR COUNTRIES (1988)	
	Total expenditure (millions of US$)
USSR	*303,000
USA	260,268
UK	22,637
France	21,903
West Germany	20,870
Japan	15,298
* 1987 figure	

INDUSTRIAL GIANT

The Japanese now turned their attention to the urgent matter of building up their economy. By providing subsidies and other support, the government promoted Japanese industries one by one, until they caught up with and overtook the rest of the world. American experts helped by teaching the Japanese how to produce better-quality goods.

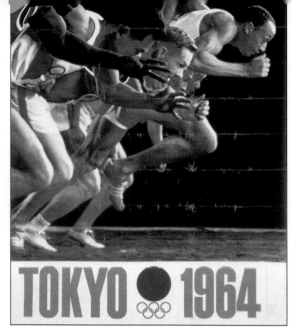

THE NATIONAL INCOME-DOUBLING PLAN

In the late 1950s there were widespread demonstrations in Japan. Many people were angry because American troops were still in the country. After a particularly violent demonstration in 1960, the prime minister, Nobusuke Kishi, was forced to resign.

The new prime minister was a man called Hayato Ikeda. He decided that if people were busy working, they would have no time to worry about politics. In 1960 he announced the national income-doubling plan. If everyone worked hard, he said, the government would help; the national income could double within ten years. His plan was astonishingly successful. In only four years the average income had doubled.

Other factors contributed to Japan's new and growing prosperity. Japan was pledged to peace. While other nations spent large amounts of money on maintaining armed forces, Japan did

In 1964, Japan hosted the Olympic Games in Tokyo. This was a symbolic event for the Japanese. It meant that they had put the war behind them and been received back into the international family of nations.

Prime Minister Hayato Ikeda, the man responsible for Japan's national income-doubling plan – and so for the country's phenomenal growth.

not. The labour force was very highly educated. And rather than spending money on research, Japan imported the latest technology from more advanced nations.

PROSPERITY AND POLLUTION

By 1964, 90 per cent of Japanese households owned a refrigerator, television and washing machine. People called them the 'three treasures'. They symbolized the new-found prosperity. But there were side effects to Japan's success. Industry was growing without any thought for the environment. Air pollution was so bad that in some highly industrialized areas the rain was black. In the 1950s, in a village called Minamata, people developed mercury poisoning from eating fish polluted btyfactory waste.

Japan's rapid growth was interrupted in 1973 when the Arab-Israeli War led to a huge rise in oil prices. Japan responded by moving away from heavy industries, which used large quantities of imported raw materials and fuels, to modern, high-technology industries such as electronics. In the second oil shock of 1979, Japan was scarcely affected.

Women assembling televisions on a modern Japanese production line. Japan's supremacy in industries such as this was one of the principal reasons for its economic success.

THE BOOM YEARS

The 1970s and 1980s were a boom time in Japan. Thanks to the development of Japanese industry and exports, the country was more prosperous than ever before. Nearly everyone enjoyed a share of the wealth. The standard of living shot up.

By the mid-1980s, Japan was investing widely abroad. Nissan opened a car factory in Sunderland, in the north of England, and another in Tennessee, in the USA. As the yen

13

The open-air cafe outside the Rockefeller Centre in New York city. This famous US landmark was bought in the 1980s by a Japanese company.

rose in value against the dollar, the Japanese were able to buy more and more foreign land and goods. Japanese companies astonished the world by buying Western art for staggeringly high prices. One company paid a record price of $82.5 million for a painting called *A Portrait of Doctor Gachet* by Vincent Van Gogh.

By the end of the 1980s the Japanese were making a third of all the world's cars, steel and ships; two-thirds of all the computer chips and consumer electronic products; and more than half the robots and machine tools installed in the world's factories. The economy continued to grow and grow.

ECONOMIC DOWNTURN

In 1989, Emperor Hirohito died. In many ways it was the end of an era. He had come to the throne in 1926 and ruled through the war years and the years of regrowth. His son, Akihito, succeeded him.

Problems were beginning to arise in Japan. Everyone had assumed that the economy would grow for ever. But in fact it began to slow down. Companies began to lose money. It was the beginning of a recession. As life grew harder, it became clear that big changes were needed, in the political system and in the economy. In 1993 the Liberal Democratic Party (LDP), which had been in power since 1955, was voted out and replaced by a reforming coalition government headed by Prime Minister Morihiro Hosokawa. In 1994 Hosokawa was replaced by Tsutomu Hata, then by Tomiichi Murayama. For Japan the era of high economic growth had passed. A new and challenging era was beginning.

Emperor Hirohito and his wife in 1953. After the Second World War, Hirohito lost all real power, but remained a figurehead for the nation until his death in 1989.

IMPORTANT DATES AND EVENTS	
1853	Commodore Perry arrives in Yokohama Bay.
1868	Meiji Restoration.
1905	Japan wins Russo-Japanese War (1904-5).
1923	Great Earthquake.
1941	Japan attacks Pearl Harbor.
1945	Japan surrenders to the Allies on 2 September.
1945-52	American occupation.
1950-53	Korean War.
1960	Prime Minister Ikeda's income-doubling plan.
1964	Tokyo Olympics.
1973	First oil shock.
1979	Second oil shock.
1989	Death of Emperor Hirohito. Accession of Emperor Akihito.
1993	LDP defeated after thirty-eight years in power.

Industry and Trade

Giant turbine blades under construction at a factory in Yokohama.

In 1952 a Japanese man named Masaru Ibuka heard about a new invention in the USA: the transistor, an electronic component which amplifies the voice. He went to the USA and paid $25,000 for a licence to develop it. He wanted to use it to make a new kind of radio. But the Americans who had invented it told him this was impossible.

Dr Ibuka named his company Sony. Two years later he had proved the Americans wrong. He developed the first transistor radios and by 1958 he was exporting them to the USA.

INDUSTRY

The secret of Japan's economic success is its phenomenal industrial growth. The government ministry responsible for overseeing the economic development of the country after the war was the Ministry of International Trade and Industry (MITI). It decided which industries to boost and allocated financial and technological aid. And to help every Japanese industry to develop, it did all it could to promote exports, while restricting imports from abroad.

But Japan's success was not due to the government alone. The Japanese people excelled in applying new ideas. Many Japanese companies – like Dr Ibuka's Sony – took products that had been invented in the West and found inspired new ways to use them.

GNP/GDP IN JAPAN

GNP (1988) : US$2,867 billion

GNP per capita (1988) : US$23,382

GDP (1991) : US$3,346,411 million

GDP per capita (1991) : US$27,005

16

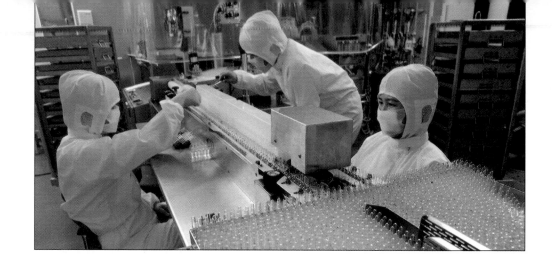

The Japanese are in the forefront of many new industries. Here medicines are being produced in sterile, high-tech laboratory conditions.

'*The driving force behind the growth of Japanese industry has been the motivation and eagerness of industry itself. Whether or not a country can pull together and wield its collective strength, at least as far as I can ascertain from Japan's case, depends more upon the initiative and fire of the people themselves than on the government.*'
– **Dr Makoto Kikuchi, Director of the Sony Research Centre, quoted in** *Inside Japan* **by Peter Tasker (Sidgwick and Jackson, 1987)**

WORLD CAR PRODUCTION (1990)		
(Figures in units of 10,000)		
Japan	1,349	27.6%
USA	978	20.0%
Germany	516	10.6%
France	377	7.7%
Italy	212	4.3%
USSR	210	4.3%
Spain	205	4.2%
Canada	193	4.0%
UK	157	3.2%
Korea	132	2.7%
Others	560	11.4%

After the war, the Japanese built up heavy industry – shipbuilding and steelmaking. Then, when that was established, they turned to consumer goods like cars, cameras, watches and televisions. After the oil crisis of 1973 they began developing high-tech industries like computing, electronics and robotics. In the 1990s they are focusing on modern industries like aerospace and biotechnology, as well as electronics.

HEAVY INDUSTRY: STEEL AND SHIPS

The steel industry is the foundation of modern Japan. Steel is essential for making ships, cars, machinery, consumer goods, even buildings. Between 1950 and 1970 steel production boomed and by 1980 Japan was the world's second-largest producer of steel. Shipbuilding was another success story. Many shipyards had survived the war and many engineers had been trained during wartime. With the help of government subsidies, the industry rapidly modernized. By 1956, Japan was producing more ships than any other country. However, in recent years both steelmaking and shipbuilding have declined, partly because of the oil crises in 1973 and 1979.

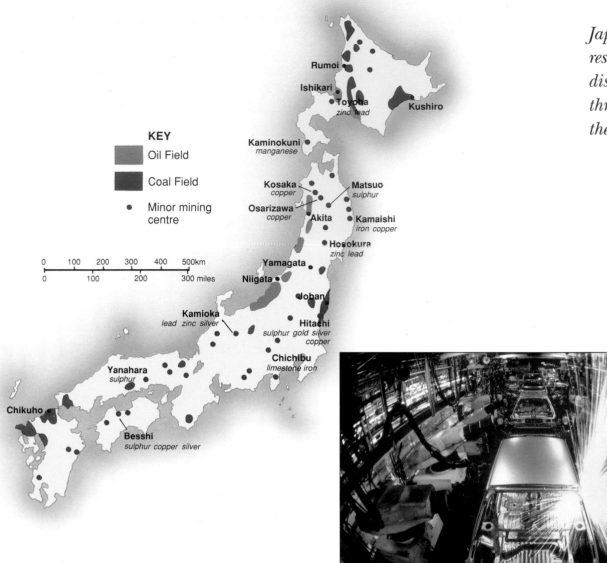

KEY

Oil Field

Coal Field

• Minor mining centre

Rumoi

Ishikari

Toyoha
zinc lead

Kushiro

Kaminokuni
manganese

Kosaka
copper

Matsuo
sulphur

Osarizawa
copper

Akita

Kamaishi
iron copper

Hosokura
zinc lead

Yamagata

Niigata

Joban

Kamioka
lead zinc silver

Hitachi
sulphur gold silver copper

Chichibu
limestone iron

Yanahara
sulphur

Chikuho

Besshi
sulphur copper silver

0 100 200 300 400 500km

0 100 200 300 miles

The steel and shipbuilding industries also face stiff competition from newly developing countries like Korea.

THE MOTOR INDUSTRY

The motor industry is one of Japan's great triumphs. Before the war it was a very minor industry. In 1950 the Japanese made a total of 1,600 motor vehicles. By 1980 they were making 11 million, more than the USA. Today Japan has the largest motor industry in the world, producing a total of about 13.5 million cars, buses and lorries every year. About half of these are exported, mainly to North America and Europe.

Robots are used to carry out many routine tasks in Japanese factories. Here they are welding steel car bodies on a production line.

18

The Honda Success Story

During the Second World War, an enthusiastic young man named Soichiro Honda ran a small company making engine parts for aeroplanes. After the war he needed to find a new way of applying his skills. Exhausted by cycling around Tokyo looking for parts and materials, he took a small 50cc engine that the army had used during the war and fixed it on to his bicycle. 'That was the first motor-powered bicycle to be made after the war,' he recalls. From there he went on to develop efficient, high-quality motorcycle manufacture.

Soichiro was not content to stop there. He wanted to make cars, too. At the time, industrial development was tightly regulated by the Ministry of International Trade and Industry (MITI). Toyota and Nissan were already making cars; MITI wanted Honda to stick to motorcycles. But Honda ignored them. Today Honda ranks alongside Toyota and Nissan as one of Japan's automobile giants. In all, Japanese companies produce almost 30 per cent of the world's cars, more than any other country. (The USA produces 20 per cent and the UK 3.2 per cent.)

At the Honda works just outside Tokyo, much of the part-making and car assembly is done by robots. The staff, all clad in hard hats, grey overalls and white gloves, work with impressive precision and speed. The small teams are trained to be flexible, so that each person can do many different jobs and produce many different models. The result is that a job such as changing a mould, which can take as much as 2 hours in an American or British factory, takes just 6 minutes.

A Honda motor-racing car.

ELECTRONICS

The oil crisis spurred Japan into developing industries that made use of human skill and knowledge rather than scarce natural resources. Today, as a result, Japanese electronic

19

goods are in demand all over the world. Japanese inventions, such as the video recorder and the Sony Walkman, have transformed everyone's lives. The output is immense. In 1991 Japan produced 26 million video recorders, 25 million cameras, 11.8 million camcorders and 3.2 million computers. 80 per cent of microchips, the tiny 'brains' that power nearly all modern electronic equipment, from digital watches to missile guidance systems, are made in Japan. In recent years, Japanese scientists have been working on high-definition television, with its super-sharp images and digital technology.

Looking down into the centre of one of Japan's nuclear power stations. Because it has to import most of the coal and oil it uses, Japan is turning to nuclear power as a more dependable energy source.

20

ROBOTICS

Like Sony's transistor radios, robotics were invented in the USA, but put to best use by the Japanese. Today industrial robots do many of the repetitive, dirty and dangerous jobs in factories, leaving human workers to carry out more skilled work. There are more than 250,000 industrial robots working in Japan, well over half the world total.

NEW TECHNOLOGY

Japanese companies now spend huge amounts on research and development. As a result, Japan has overtaken the USA in lasers, video, digital electronics and semi-conductors (electronic devices such as transistors). And Japanese companies are competing successfully with European and American firms to develop the newest industries such as biotechnology.

Although it is a small country, Japan has a large share of international trade.

WORLD TRADE SHARE OF MAJOR COUNTRIES	
USA	14.88%
Germany	11.09%
Japan	10.43%
Others	63.60%

Morning exercises in company uniform are a feature of many Japanese businesses. Here, employees of Toyota work out.

LIFE AT WORK

For the Japanese far more than for most other people, life revolves around work. About 30 per cent of the workforce belongs to one of the large companies such as Sony, Toshiba or Nissan. They are part of the lifetime employment system. These companies are like large families. Once you have joined, you stay with the company for life. The company takes care of you. It provides housing, health care, schooling for your children, even your annual holiday. It guarantees you a job for life, with a regular rise in pay. In exchange the company expects hard work and loyalty.

Within the company, every worker is valued. The day begins very early. Usually there are physical exercises, followed by a meeting to discuss the day's work. Everyone can contribute their opinion and everyone's views are respected. Within the factory or office, everyone wears the same uniform or suit, no matter what his or her position. And at noon, managing directors and workers eat in the same canteen.

In the evening, office workers often go out together to a bar. For any ambitious young man, it is vital to socialize with workmates and bosses. It would be unusual to get back from work much before midnight.

IMPORTS (1990)

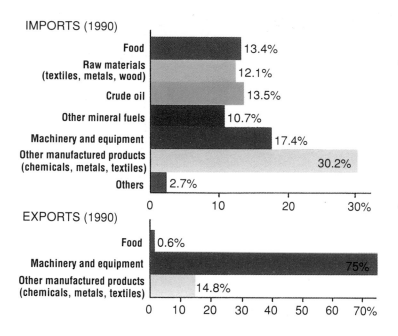

Food 13.4%
Raw materials (textiles, metals, wood) 12.1%
Crude oil 13.5%
Other mineral fuels 10.7%
Machinery and equipment 17.4%
Other manufactured products (chemicals, metals, textiles) 30.2%
Others 2.7%

EXPORTS (1990)

Food 0.6%
Machinery and equipment 75%
Other manufactured products (chemicals, metals, textiles) 14.8%

TRADE

Japanese products reach all parts of the world in vast quantities. All our homes and offices are full of Japanese goods, from electronic games, televisions and video recorders to cameras, cars and computers. The Japanese have perfected the art of making high-quality goods which everyone wants and which are sold everywhere at competitive prices.

Japan's economic success is based on trade. It earns far more from exports than it spends on imports. In 1991 it earned $314,500 million from exports and spent $236,700 million on imports. This gap is called the trade surplus and Japan has the largest ever known.

One reason for the gap is that there are controls limiting imports to Japan. These were first set up after the war, when the Japanese economy was weak and needed protection. Now the Americans are putting pressure on Japan to allow more foreign goods into the country.

This chart highlights Japan's dependence on fuels from abroad and its success in exporting manufactured goods.

Japan's financial success is reflected in the power of the Tokyo Stock Exchange. Long before markets in London and New York open for business, Tokyo may have bought and sold millions of shares and transformed the economic situation worldwide.

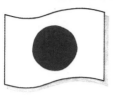

Life on the Land

Until 100 years ago Japan was a nation of farmers. Now agriculture is in decline. Ever since the economic boom began, young people have been leaving the countryside and moving to the cities, where they can find work that is less strenuous and better paid than farming. Today in many villages in the countryside only old people remain. In fact 63 per cent of the farming population is over 55 years old.

Japanese farms are very small, usually only 1 or 2 hectares in area. This is small enough for one farmer to work alone. Rice is the main crop. It is grown in paddy fields which have to be specially dug out and carefully irrigated. In the past, rice farming was a full-time job. Nowadays there are mechanical planters for planting out the rice seedlings in the spring, harvesters for harvesting them in the autumn, fertilizers and weedkillers. As a result, farming takes only two weeks a year. Most farmers have another job. In many families the old people take care of the rice fields while the young people go out to work in offices or factories.

'The superiority of Japan over other countries, observed an 18th-century historian, Motoori Norinaga, could be simply demonstrated by the quality of its rice, which surpassed that grown elsewhere. Rice was sacred and represented the soul of the nation. Many Japanese . . . have said much the same ever since.'
– **'Going against the grain in Japan',** *The Economist,* **23 April 1994**

Harvesting rice near Kyoto on the island of Honshu. The use of machinery in agriculture has revolutionized farming in Japan. Now far fewer workers are needed.

Rice was once the staple food of Japan, eaten at every meal. The word for 'a meal' in Japanese is in fact the same as the word for 'rice'. But tastes are changing. Today people eat less rice and more Western foods like bread, meat and dairy products. More rice is grown than can be sold. The government buys rice from farmers at an artificially high price to protect the farmer's incomes and then sells it to consumers. The price of rice in Japan today is up to seven times the price on the world market.

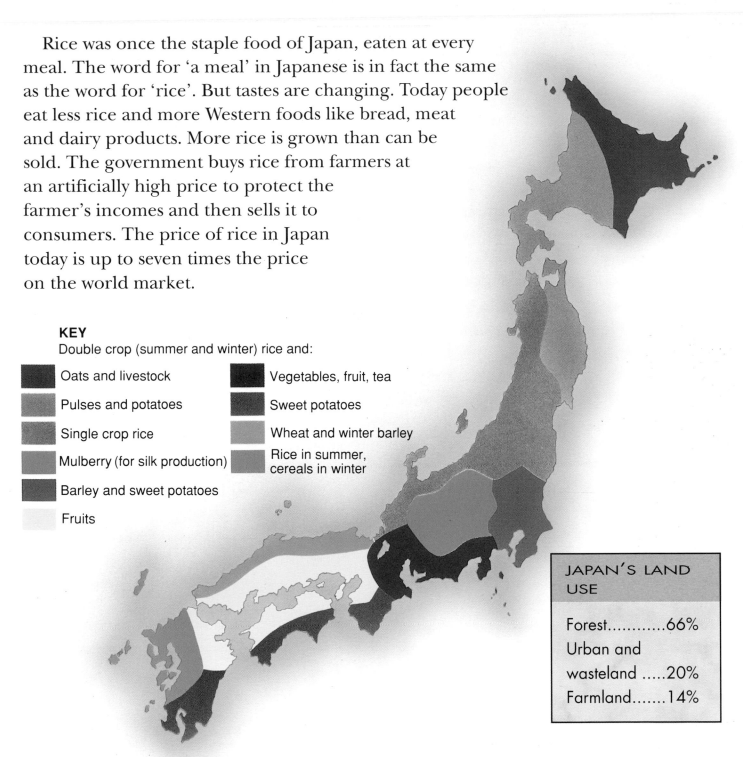

KEY

Double crop (summer and winter) rice and:

Oats and livestock

Pulses and potatoes

Single crop rice

Mulberry (for silk production)

Barley and sweet potatoes

Fruits

Vegetables, fruit, tea

Sweet potatoes

Wheat and winter barley

Rice in summer, cereals in winter

JAPAN'S LAND USE

Forest............66%
Urban and wasteland 20%
Farmland.......14%

Rice is grown throughout Japan, but farms also produce other important crops.

Besides rice, major crops include tomatoes, aubergines, carrots, sweet potatoes, onions, water melons and strawberries. Apples and pears are grown in the cool north. Tea, mandarin oranges, tangerines, peaches and nectarines are grown in the south. In all, Japan produces about 50 per cent of the food it needs. This consists largely of rice, vegetables and fruit. Other foods, like wheat and soya beans, have to be supplemented by imports.

Tradition and Change

Toshimasa Kuronuma lives in the village of Yamanouchi, in a beautiful valley surrounded by steep, tree-clad hills, about 400 kilometres north of Tokyo. When he was 20 he went to Tokyo for a few years. But he knew that when his father grew old he would come back to be the head of the household and take care of the family land.

In the traditional way, four generations of the family live together under the same roof. Toshimasa's grandmother was born in 1910 and has lived in this house all her married life. She still remembers the days when

the only lighting was by oil lamp, and in the winter, when the snow was 3 metres deep, everyone stayed at home, huddled around the charcoal brazier. Like his grandmother,

A circular rice field and family house in the mountainous Takayama region on the island of Honshu, central Japan.

MEAT AND FISH

The most dramatic change in the Japanese diet is the eating of meat. In the past, the Japanese followed Buddhist precepts which forbade meat-eating. Now many popular dishes, such as *sukiyaki*, are made with beef. Every city has several branches of McDonald's.

Many beef cattle are kept on the pastureland of Hokkaido. But the beef Japanese like best comes from cattle reared underground near Kobe, in central Japan. They are fed on beer, sprayed with sake and given a daily massage to knead the fat through their muscles.

Toshimasa's mother came from a neighbouring family, and after her arranged marriage spent her time cooking, cleaning and caring for her in-laws. Toshimasa, however, is different. He and his wife Emiko married for love. They have three children: a boy, Daisuke, and a girl, Akiko, who both attend the village school, and a baby.

While his father works in the family rice fields, Toshimasa has brought industry to the village. He has a small workshop in a lean-to near his house where several of the village women work, stamping shoe uppers out of sheets of leather. In the evening Emiko cooks and the family sit around together watching television or a video. Like most boys,

The Japanese eat a great variety of fish. Roast tai (sea bream) are always served at weddings and New Year celebrations.

Daisuke is fascinated by computers. While his father, Toshimasa, came back to live in the village, Daisuke is already talking about starting a new life in Tokyo.

As an island country, the Japanese have always eaten a great deal of fish and products of the sea such as seaweed. The traditional Japanese diet consisted of rice and fish with vegetables. Japanese still eat three times as much fish as meat. Japanese fishing fleets trawl the ocean for tuna, cod, sardines and other fish, while smaller boats fish off the coast for mackerel and prawns. Whale meat is also popular, although now there is a ban on whale hunting.

Fish farming is a good way to increase the crop of fish. Saltwater fish like yellowtail tuna and sea bream are reared in sheltered bays, while eels, carp, trout and other

The old methods of farming have not completely died out. In some areas, rice seedlings are still planted by hand, an immensely time-consuming task.

freshwater fish are kept in large ponds and harvested when mature. The Japanese enjoy many varieties of edible seaweed. Laver seaweed (*nori*) is grown in Kyushu, while kelp (*kombu*) is gathered around the coast of Hokkaido.

RURAL DEVELOPMENT

Although incomes in the country are lower than those in the cities, rural families have also benefited from Japan's economic miracle. Most have the modern conveniences, such as cars, televisions, video recorders and stereos. And because there is more space, houses in the countryside are often larger than those in the city.

In recent years the government has become concerned about the flow of population from the countryside to the

INTERNATIONAL RICE PRICES (1991)	
Price paid to producers for 1 tonne unhulled rice (Prices are in US$)	
Japan	1,537
USA	236
Thailand	164
Price paid by consumers for 1 kilogram polished rice	
Japan	2.71
USA	1.10
Thailand	0.44

cities. In 1960, the farming population was 13.4 million, 30.2 per cent of the total workforce. By 1990 it was only 4 million, 6.4 per cent of the workforce. In order to reverse this trend they have begun relocating industries to country areas, to provide work for the people there.

As Japan becomes increasingly prosperous, people are able to enjoy more leisure time. In 1987 the government passed a law to encourage the development of resorts in rural areas. With government assistance, many construction firms are turning mountain regions into ski resorts and golf courses. But some people are opposed to this. They fear that large parts of the countryside may be destroyed.

The beauty of Mount Fuji obscured by a modern chemical plant. In recent years, the Japanese have made great efforts to pursue industrial growth without spoiling the countryside.

FOOD SELF-SUFFICIENCY OF MAJOR COUNTRIES (1988)

Japan	49%
UK*	73%
Germany	94%
USA	113%
France	143%

* 1987 figure

Today there is greater concern about the environment than ever before. In the early days after the Second World War, development was such an urgent matter that little care was taken of the countryside. Electric cables stretched from mountain to mountain, pylons sprouted on the mountainsides, and riverbanks and hillsides were lined with concrete to prevent erosion of the soil. Now the Japanese are trying to reverse the damage that has been done to their beautiful country.

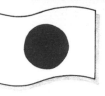

People and Society

When they visit Japan, many people feel that they are stepping into the world of the future. Its cities are full of steel and glass, skyscrapers, dazzling neon, shiny new cars and well-dressed people. It is the country of Nintendo, of Sony, Toshiba, Nikon and Honda. Most Japanese have a fax machine, a laptop computer, and cable and satellite television in their homes.

All this is the result of Japan's economic miracle. Yet beneath the surface, the way that people lead their lives is altering much more slowly.

Two Japanese punks.

A CHANGING SOCIETY

A hundred years ago the Japanese lived in large extended families, with grandparents, parents and children all together under one roof. Marriages were usually arranged by a matchmaker and when the eldest son married, his new wife came to live with the family. Women were almost like servants: when the men ate, the women stayed in the kitchen. Most people did the same job as their father. Few ever moved away from the place where they were born.

'*A Japanese punk will be clean, friendly and, almost certainly, bound for the respectable life of a white-shirted salary-man marching between office and noodle shop in Marunouchi and bowing to an alarmingly acute angle even when talking on the phone to a superior. He and most of his friends will always, finally, answer the call of duty, the call of Japan.*'
– **Bryan Appleyard, *The Independent*, 25 May 1994**

Today many Japanese have moved to the cities in search of freedom from the old family system, as well as to find work. In the vast, crowded cities, land is so expensive that most people cannot even think of owning their own homes. Instead they live in cramped rented apartments. Here there is no space for grandparents, so people live in small nuclear families – mother, father and just one or two children.

In the past nearly everyone married in Japan. If you did not meet a suitable partner yourself, your parents would arrange one for you. People used to say that once a woman's 25th birthday had passed, she was too old and would be left on the shelf.

The vast majority of people still marry. Divorce is far less common than in Europe and the USA. But very recently, young working women have begun to rebel against this custom. More and more are choosing not to marry. Today women have far greater opportunities than they have ever had before. 38 per cent of the workforce are women. Although Japan still lags behind Europe and the USA, increasing numbers of high-level managerial posts there are becoming available to women.

One growing problem for Japan is the change in the population balance. Women are having fewer children. In 1930 the average number of children per household was 4.7, whereas now it is 1.5. But while the number of young people is falling, the number of old people is growing. Thanks to better diet and health care, everyone is living longer. Japan has the longest life expectancy in the world. While the workforce grows smaller, the number of people to be supported grows larger and larger. It is a problem that all the developed countries will soon have to confront. Japan is the first to face it and is already looking for solutions.

WOMEN IN THE WORKFORCE (1990)	
Japan	38%
UK	40%
USA	43%
USSR	51%

Modern Japanese women like these two young designers are gradually making their mark in the workplace. But they have yet to catch up with their counterparts in the West.

LIFE EXPECTANCY (1991)	
Males	76 years
Females	82 years

31

Minority Views

If you walk the streets of Tokyo, the vast majority of faces around you are Japanese; there is very little racial diversity. There are however several minority groups in Japan. They generally suffer discrimination, particularly in the areas of employment and marriage.

BURAKUMIN

In the time of the shoguns, the *burakumin*, 'community people', were the outcasts who performed jobs considered to be unclean, like animal slaughter and leather work. Ethnically, they were and are pure Japanese, indistinguishable from 'ordinary' Japanese. Today they have full legal rights; but in fact they still suffer discrimination. There are 2 to 3 million *burakumin*. Most live in ghettoes around Osaka and in the west of Japan. Their origin is a problem if they apply for a job in a large company or wish to marry outside the *buraku* community. If prospective employers or in-laws check their family records and discover that they are *burakumin*, they are likely to be turned down. There are many activist groups, such as the Burakumin Liberation League, fighting for equal rights.

KOREANS

There are fewer than 1 million foreign residents of Japan and the vast majority of these – about 80 per cent – are Korean; in 1990 there were 687,940. Many come from families that were forcibly brought to Japan to be labourers and factory workers during the Japanese occupation of Korea between 1910 and 1945. Most were born and raised in Japan and speak only Japanese. Yet they are denied full citizenship and instead are classed as 'permanent residents'. They have no vote and are forced to carry identification cards at all times, and to be fingerprinted.

AINU

The Ainu were the original inhabitants of Hokkaido. Before the Japanese occupied the island in the early nineteenth century, they had their own culture, which was akin to that of the Inuit. They had their own

'You will feel disgust and loathing for me now that I have told you what I am. But though I was born so low myself, I have done my best each day to teach you only what is right and true. Please remember this, and forgive me if you can for having kept the truth from you till today. When you get home, tell your parents what I have said. Tell them that I confessed today, asking your forgiveness. I am an eta (burakumin), an outcast, an unclean being!'
– A *burakumin* teacher who had concealed his origins, confessing to his pupils. From *The Broken Commandment* by Toson Shimazaki (1906)

language and literature, made dug-out canoes and lived in thatched houses; the women tattooed their hands and lips. They were taller than the Japanese, with more hair, stronger features and sometimes blue eyes. Today there are very few pure Ainu left, officially between 18,000 and 25,000, though many people in Hokkaido are of mixed blood. Ainu culture and language have practically died out, and are preserved only as a tourist attraction in a few rather sad villages. In general, the Ainu have lower incomes and a lower standard of living than other Japanese. However, there are now Ainu activist groups who have instilled a new sense of pride.

FOREIGN WORKERS

Japanese are so well educated that few need or want to do factory work or manual labour. In recent years foreign workers from neighbouring Asian countries have entered Japan, often illegally, in search of higher wages. They now form a sizeable minority. They carry out essential work, often live in considerable poverty and are perpetually at risk of deportation. The Japanese government, realizing that the country needs these workers, has begun to consider amending immigration procedures.

Left   Akankohan on the shores of Lake Akan in Hokkaido is one of the few remaining Ainu villages.

Foreign workers in Japan are beginning to fight for legal status and better living and working conditions.

MODERN AND TRADITIONAL SIDE BY SIDE

During the Second World War, every Japanese city except one – the historic city of Kyoto – was flattened by Allied bombs. As a result there are few old buildings left in the country. The cities were rebuilt very quickly and some are very ugly. But as Japan has become more prosperous, many spectacular examples of modern architecture have sprung up. Architects from Europe and the USA have gone to Japan to design buildings which express some of their most radical ideas.

The extraordinary Flamme d'or building in Asakusa, Tokyo. It was designed by French architect Philippe Starck, one of several Western architects to work in Japan during the 1980s boom years.

But while Japanese cities are full of modern buildings, and people go to work in modern offices, at home most still enjoy living in the traditional style. Floors are covered with sweet-smelling straw *tatami* matting. People remove their shoes when they enter the house, and at night sleep on futons, thin mattresses which are spread on the floor.

The most popular sport in Japan first arrived with the coming of the Americans around 1870. It is baseball. Every Japanese schoolboy plays the game, and in the summer everyone follows the progress of the two major leagues, the Central League and the Pacific League. But the Japanese have transformed baseball and made it a very different game from the American one.

The Japanese call baseball yakyu, and it is a national passion. Inter-school competitions allow enthusiasts to participate from an early age.

Soccer is also growing in popularity. In 1992 the English player Gary Lineker moved to Japan to become one of the stars of the J (for 'Japanese') League. Japan is hoping to host the World Cup in 2002.

Along with modern sports, people also enjoy traditional ones. Sumo is considered not a sport but the national skill. The huge sumo wrestlers are national heroes. The largest of them all, Konishiki, weighs 230 kilograms. The current Grand Champion is the American-born wrestler Akebono. People also practise sports like judo, and kendo, a form of sword-fighting.

The traditional Japanese sport of sumo wrestling began in the third century AD. The huge wrestlers, called rikishi, fight on the dohyo, a raised area in the centre of an arena.

WORK AND LEISURE

For the generation that survived the war, the most essential thing was to rebuild their country. Everyone worked as hard as they could. They saved money and led quiet lives. But by the 1980s a new generation of Japanese was growing up. The Japan they knew was prosperous. Like their parents they expected to work, but they also expected to spend the money they earnt on enjoying life.

Over the last ten years, working time in Japan has decreased and time spent on leisure activities has increased.

35

One of the most important modern industries in Japan is the leisure industry. Every weekend in winter the trains are crowded with young Japanese going to the mountains to ski. There are also many health clubs in Japan where old people exercise beside young ones.

Another new trend is the large numbers of Japanese going on foreign holidays. The yen is now very strong. A few yen will buy a large amount of dollars or pounds. This makes foreign travel affordable for practically everyone in Japan. Since 1980 the number of people going abroad has more than doubled.

The Ginza district of Tokyo is a busy centre of shopping and commerce. But the Japanese recession has hit consumer spending power hard and department stores no longer make the spectacular profits of the 1980s.

CONSUMER SOCIETY

As Japan has become richer, it has turned into a throw-away society. Every year, in order to sell more of their goods, manufacturers produce new computers, new cars, new videos, new audio equipment. No one wants the old models, so they are simply thrown away.

By the boom years of the 1980s, shopping had become a craze. Department stores were like miniature cities. There were luxury imported foods in the basement, floors devoted to the latest high-tech products, and art galleries, concert halls and cinemas within the store.

Everyone had more money to spend. Young women with high salaries who lived with their parents had the highest disposable incomes of all. They went on shopping sprees to Hong Kong, or even Milan or Paris.

36

Learning the Language

As Japanese society changes, so does the Japanese language. There are three different scripts. The first writing system came from Chinese (though the spoken language has no relation to Chinese). Like Chinese, Japanese uses characters (*kanji*) derived originally from pictures. School children have to learn roughly 2,000 different pictorial characters in order to be basically literate; most people carry on learning new characters throughout their lives. While these Chinese characters convey basic concepts, the grammar of the sentence is written in another script, *hiragana*. *Hiragana* is an alphabet with 46 letters. In the sentence 'the cat sat on the mat', 'cat', 'to sit' and 'mat' would be in *kanji*, while the past tense of 'to sit' and the preposition 'on' would be written in *hiragana*.

The third script, *katakana*, expresses the same sounds as *hiragana* and also has 46 letters. *Katakana* is used for words of foreign, usually Western, origin –

and it is through *katakana* that Western words flood into Japanese. As Japan changes, so more and more Western words enter the language. People live in apartments (*apaato*), shop in supermarkets (*supaa*) or department stores (*depaato*), wear shirts (*shaatsu*) and ties (*nekutai*) or one-piece dresses (*wanpeesu*), operate their word processors (*waapuro*) or watch television (*terebi*), and sleep in beds (*beddo*). At the weekend they play golf (*gorufu*) or go hiking (*haikingu*). With all these Western words, Japanese is not as difficult to learn as people think!

A young child copying kanji characters on to a blackboard.

With the coming of the 1990s and the economic downturn, people have become more cautious. They are spending much less and department stores are beginning to suffer enormous losses.

Japanese high school boys on a trip to the Heian shrine in Kyoto. Military-style uniforms are common for this age group.

Japanese schools are generally very well equipped. Here a mixed class works in a specially designed computer room.

EDUCATION

The Japanese are probably the most highly educated people in the world. Their compulsory nine-year education starts at 5, but 8 out of 10 children go to kindergarten from the age of 3. Primary school lasts for six years and middle school for three years. Nearly everyone goes on to senior high school and 1 in 3 go to university.

At school everyone works extremely hard. The Japanese language itself takes many years to learn. Children have homework from primary school and there is a great deal of pressure on students, who sit exams all the way through school. If they fail, they have to repeat the year. Many go to extra classes in the evenings to help them get through.

The most important exam of all is the university entrance exam. There are 514 universities in Japan, of which 136 are public, 378 private and fee-paying. Those who graduate from one of the best universities are guaranteed a job in one of the country's best companies.

The Kinkakuji Temple (Golden Pavilion) in the ancient city of Kyoto, Kyoto was the capital of Japan from 794-1868 AD,

CRIME

Japan is one of the safest countries in the world, with an exceptionally low crime rate. In 1988, there were just 1,161.21 crimes for every 100,000 people, compared with almost five times as many in the UK and USA. There is, however, a lot of organized crime, which is run by the *yakuza*, the Japanese equivalent of the Mafia.

RELIGION

Shinto is the most ancient religion in Japan. According to Shinto, there are gods everywhere. Mountains, rocks, trees and rivers are all gods; and we too become gods when we die. Shinto gods take care of us while we are alive. Schoolchildren pray for success in exams and business-men pray for success in their work. But when people get old they pray to the Buddha. In Japan, Buddhist priests carry out funerals and keep the ashes of the dead.

Japan has 96 million Buddhists, 109 million followers of Shinto, 1.5 million Christians and 10 million followers of other religions – which adds up to far more than the population of Japan (124 million). Most Japanese see no problem in believing in more than one religion.

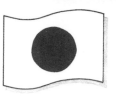

Communications and Transport

The Japanese often have to travel long distances, but transport is extremely fast and efficient. In fact Japan probably has the most efficient communications network in the world. The four main islands and thousands of smaller islands are linked by road, railway, ferry and aeroplane.

For long distances, most people use the train. Japan pioneered high-speed trains in the 1960s and the *Shinkansen* or 'Bullet Train' is justifiably famous. For many years it was

The dramatic sight of a Bullet Train hurtling past Japanese mountains at about 275 kilometres an hour.

the fastest train in the world, although today it has been overtaken by the French TGV.

Bullet Train lines run the length of Honshu, from Morioka in the north to Fukuoka at the top of the southern island of Kyushu. Each year faster trains are developed. The fastest train at the moment covers the 553 kilometres between Tokyo and Osaka in 2½ hours, travelling at 275 kilometres an hour. Bullet Trains depart every 3 or 4 minutes. Like all Japanese transport, they are so punctual that you can set your watch by them. Within the cities there are local trains, underground trains and buses. All are extremely punctual.

Travelling by road is the least efficient form of transport. Motorways crisscross above Tokyo and are so crowded that often the traffic is not moving at all. Many people have bicycles and use them to cycle to the station.

Tunnels and bridges join Japan's four main islands. The Seikan Tunnel between Honshu and Hokkaido is 43 kilometres long and the second longest tunnel in the world after the Channel Tunnel between England and France (50 kilometres). The longest suspension bridge in the world is currently under construction. It will be 1,990 metres long and link the islands of Honshu and Shikoku.

Distances in Japan are deceptively large. From Morioka in the north to Fukuoka in the south takes 10 hours, even on the high-speed Bullet Train. Many people prefer to fly and there is a well-developed network of internal flights. Japan is the only country in the world that uses jumbo jets for internal flights, because there are so many passengers.

NEW NETWORKS

At the moment an important part of the Japanese government's programme is to develop the rural areas by relocating industry in distant part of the country, far from the major cities. To do this successfully, they want to ensure that every parts of the country is linked to the communications network. The government has plans to build a network of airports, motorways and Bullet Train

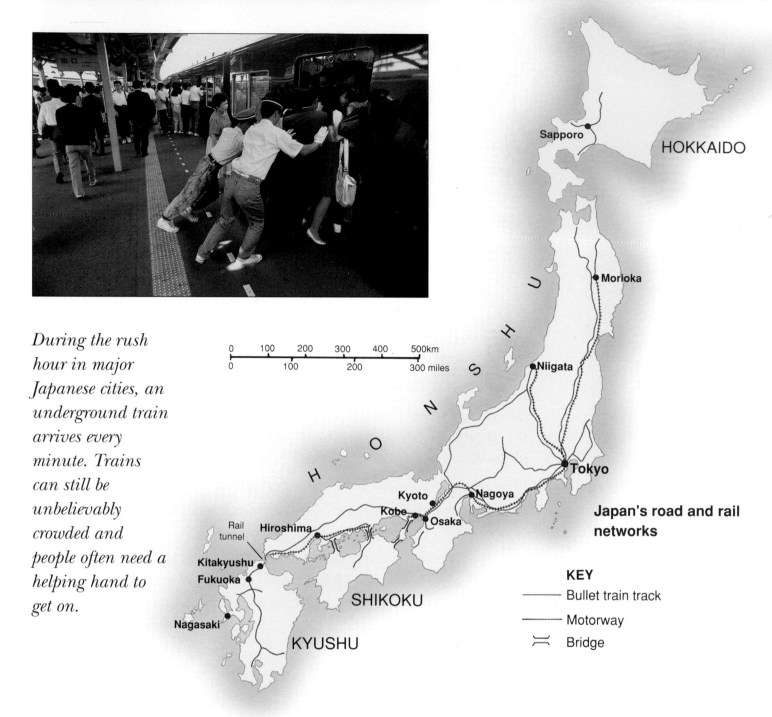

During the rush hour in major Japanese cities, an underground train arrives every minute. Trains can still be unbelievably crowded and people often need a helping hand to get on.

Japan's road and rail networks

KEY
———— Bullet train track
———— Motorway
⟩⟨ Bridge

Japan's major land transport networks.

lines to make every part of Japan accessible within a travelling time of 90 minutes.

Many building works connected with this plan are already under way. In 1994 the Kansai International Airport will open, on an artificial island off the coast near Osaka. Other islands are being built at different locations around the country. One, near Nagoya, will hold the Chubu International Airport. Several will be built in Tokyo Bay, with a highway across the bay linking the islands. This work should be complete by the late 1990s.

INFORMATION REVOLUTION

In Japan the information revolution has meant that people no longer need to meet to do business. Nearly every household in Japan has a telephone. Many private homes also have fax machines. In 1991 4.3 million fax machines were manufactured, twice as many as in 1988. Some people, worried about the prospect of an earthquake destroying Tokyo, live outside the city and conduct their business by fax.

Japanese computer screens show a mixture of icons and Japanese-language instructions.

Even more sophisticated means of communication are becoming available. People who have cable television can use it for home banking and home shopping. Products are advertised on the television screen and customers simply phone up and order them. ISDNs (integrated services digital networks) link telephone, fax, cable television and other media into one network.

The Japanese are also developing CD-ROMs (compact disc-read only memories). With these, a single compact disc can hold all the information from a large dictionary or a library catalogue. IC (integrated circuit) cards have made it possible to develop compact electronic dictionaries. Many people now own language dictionaries and even slim electronic diaries which use IC cards.

This five-way telephone system allows conference calls to be held between people in five different locations. The callers can see one another on a television screen at the same time.

43

Facing the Future

Today Tokyo is the capital of the world's wealthiest and most highly industrialized nation. Japan is like a banker to the rest of the world and the world's ten largest banks are all Japanese. While Japan lends money, other countries borrow it. Many countries, including the USA, are in debt to Japan.

ECONOMIC DOWNTURN

In the early 1990s, Japan's economic growth began to slow. People stopped buying so many expensive goods. As a result, some shopkeepers began to lose money. Now, some companies are closing down, building projects are being cancelled. Until the downturn began, there was almost no unemployment at all. Now a few people are losing their jobs. Despite this. compared with other countries the Japanese are still a prosperous nation.

PRESSURES FROM ABROAD

Some of the greatest pressures on Japan's future come from outside the country. Despite Japan's enormous prosperity, its industries are still protected against imported foreign goods, as they were at the end of the war. Japan itself, however, can export freely. Many countries regard this as unfair and have in their turn set limits on the number of Japanese goods they are willing to import. For years the USA in particular has put pressure on Japan to import more foreign goods, especially rice. Recent trade talks have

Homeless men sleeping on Tokyo's streets. Like many other countries, the recession has meant an increase in homelessness in Japan. Only when the economy improves will such problems begin to disappear.

Japan's post-war peace constitution states that the Japanese may not wage war. However, they are allowed to participate in United Nations peacekeeping forces, as they are doing here in Cambodia.

resulted in deadlock. It seems likely that the Americans will do all they can to limit imports from Japan. This is bound to have a very bad effect on the Japanese economy.

There is also pressure on Japan to take more part in international affairs. The Japanese argue that they have a peace constitution, which prevents them from taking part in warfare. But they have started playing a larger role in the United Nations. Japan also contributes more aid to developing countries than any other nation in the world.

FACING THE FUTURE

One last unknown factor affects the future of Japan. The Japanese have been expecting a huge and devastating earthquake to destroy much of Tokyo since the early 1990s. The country is now such an important economic force throughout the world that if Tokyo were badly damaged, all economies would suffer.

The Japanese have always overcome whatever difficulties lay in their path. Many people believe that in the next century the most powerful region of the world will be the Pacific Rim. Countries like China, Korea, Taiwan, Vietnam and Thailand are rapidly becoming stronger and more wealthy. But despite its current problems, Japan is still unquestionably the economic leader.

Glossary

Biotechnology   A new industry that uses biological techniques such as fermentation and genetic engineering to make drugs and other products.

Coalition   A government consisting not of a single political party but of several different parties which join together to form a majority.

Conglomerate   A group of companies linked together.

Disposable income   Money which can be spent freely after essential bills like rent, electricity, telephone and food have been subtracted.

Epicentre   The point where an earthquake starts, and which therefore suffers the strongest shocks.

Futon   Japanese bedding, both mattresses and quilts, which is laid out on the floor at night and folded up and put away in the morning.

Industrial Revolution   The transformation of Great Britain and later the rest of Europe and the USA from mainly agricultural to mainly industrial countries. This happened during the eighteenth and nineteenth centuries.

Judo   The best-known Japanese martial art. Judo is a form of wrestling which involves using an opponent's body-weight to throw him or her.

Kendo   A martial art. Kendo is a form of sword-fighting using wooden swords.

Recession   A time of economic weakness marked by a fall in the value of currency, business closures and often unemployment.

Sake   Rice wine. Sake is a sweet, clear alcoholic drink made by fermenting rice. In winter it is drunk warm, in summer, cold.

Shogun   The title of the military dictators who ruled Japan from 1603 to 1868.

Strike   A planned stoppage of work, usually to protest against bad conditions or low wages.

Sukiyaki   A very popular dish of fried beef, usually cooked at the diner's table.

Sumo   One of the most popular Japanese spectator sports. Sumo wrestlers weigh more than 100 kilograms. They try to topple their opponent or push him out of the ring.

Tatami   Thick straw mats which line the floors of traditional Japanese houses.

Yen   The currency used in Japan.

Zaibatsu   One of a group of conglomerate companies that dominated Japan's economy up to 1945 and were often controlled by one family, such as Mitsui or Mitsubishi.

Further Information

BOOKS

Non-fiction

Focus on Japan by Mavis Pilbeam (Hamish Hamilton, 1987)

A Geography of Japan by Donald MacDonald (Paul Norbury, 1985)

Inside Japan; Wealth, Work and Power in the New Japanese Empire by Peter Tasker
(Penguin Books, 1987)

Japan from Shogun to Superstate by Stuart Fewster and Tony Gorton
(Paul Norbury Publications, 1988)

Japan, Country Fact Files by John Baines (Simon & Schuster, 1992)

Nippon, New Superpower; Japan since 1945 by William Horsley & Roger Buckley
(BBC Books, 1990)

Fiction

An Artist of the Floating World by Kazuo Ishiguro is a short novel about the changes in Japan this century. It is published in paperback.

FILMS

Empire of the Sun (1987) An English boy living in Japanese-occupied Shanghai in the late 1930s is fascinated by the Japanese soldiers, pilots and aircraft he sees around him. When the Second World War breaks out he is separated from his parents and imprisoned by the Japanese. At the end of the war, the family is reunited.

Tampopo (1986) The story of a woman who sets out to make the best noodle bar in Japan, helped by her country-and-western-loving truck driver friend.

PICTURE ACKNOWLEDGEMENTS

Eye Ubiquitous 14, 19, 22, 24, 27, 35 top left, 37, 38 top; Robert Harding 30; The Hulton-Deutsch Collection Limited 7 left, 8, 9, 11, 12 bottom, 15; Rex features Limited 12 top, 17, 31, 45; Tony Stone Worldwide 3, 4 left and right, 6 centre left, 7 right, 10, 13, 16, 18, 20-21, 23, 28, 35 centre right, 36, 38 right, 39, 40-41, 42, 44; Topham Picture Source 6 top left, 26, 29, 32, 43 bottom; Zul/Chapel Studios 33, 34, 43 top.

Maps were provided by Peter Bull.

Index

The figures in **bold** refer to photographs and maps.